Amalfi Coast Iconic Travel Guide 2024

Exploring Positano, Ravello, Sorrento, Must-see Attraction, Travel Tips, Exciting Activities, Hidden Treasures in Naples, Reference MAP

Tara D. Hayes

Copyright © 2024 by Tara D. Hayes

All rights reserved. No part of this publication may be reproduced, distributed, or transmitted in any form or by any means, including photocopying, recording, or other electronic or mechanical methods, without the prior written permission of the publisher, except for brief quotations in critical reviews and certain other noncommercial uses permitted by copyright law.

This book is a non-fiction work. All characters, incidents, and dialogue are based on the author's personal experiences, interviews, and research. Any resemblance to actual persons, living or dead, or events is purely coincidental.

While every effort has been made to provide accurate and up-to-date information, neither the author nor the publisher can be held liable for any errors or omissions or for any consequences resulting from the use of this information.

Table of Contents

Part 1: Introduction. 5

    Chapter 1: Welcome to Paradise: An Introduction to the Amalfi Coast. 6

    Chapter 2: Brief History of the Amalfi Coast 9

    Chapter 3: When To Visit The Amalfi Coast (Weather, Seasons, and Crowds) 13

Part 2: Plan Your Trip 18

    Chapter 4: Getting There and Around (Flights, Ferries, Buses, and Car Rentals) 19

    Chapter 5: Where to Stay (Choosing an Amalfi Coast Town) 23

    Chapter 6: What to Pack (The Essentials for Your Amalfi Coast Adventure) 28

Part 3: Must-See Towns and Villages 32

    Chapter 7: Positano, the Pearl of the Amalfi Coast. 33

    Chapter 8: Amalfi: History and Culture in a Picturesque Setting. 39

    Chapter 9: Ravello: Hilltop Paradise with Stunning Views. 42

    Chapter 10: Sorrento, a lively gateway to the Amalfi Coast. 46

    Chapter 11: Hidden Gems: Exploring Smaller Towns (Praiano, Furore, and Atrani 49

Part 4: Activities and Experiences. 56

   Chapter 12: Hiking the Amalfi Coast: Stunning Trails and Panoramic Views 57

   Chapter 13: Beach Activities: Sunbathing, Swimming, and Water Sports. 60

   Chapter 14: Boating Adventures: Exploring the Coastline at Sea 63

   Chapter 15: Cultural Highlights: Museums, Churches, and Historic Sites 66

   Chapter 16: Foodie Paradise: Amalfi Coast Cuisine and Cooking Classes. 71

Part 5: Practical Information. 74

   Chapter 17: Budgeting Your Trip (Costs, Transportation, and Accommodation) 75

   Chapter 18: Language and Communication (Essential Italian Phrases). 79

   Chapter 19: Staying Safe and Healthy (Tips and Medical Care) 82

Part Six: Appendix 85

   Appendix A: Festival and Event Calendar 85

   Appendix B: Maps of the Amalfi Coast. 88

Part 1: Introduction.

Chapter 1: Welcome to Paradise: An Introduction to the Amalfi Coast.

Close your eyes for a minute. Imagine blue seas so transparent that you can see the stones on the seafloor. Now, open them; that's the Amalfi coast. Pastel-colored buildings flow down stunning cliffs and hang dangerously to the slope. The hills are covered in lush vineyards, and the air is rich with the aroma of lemons mixed with salty spray. This is your first introduction to heaven.

A Living Piece of History.

The Amalfi Coast is more than simply a collection of breathtaking views. History whispers from every cobblestone street. Follow along the footsteps of merchants and conquerors from ages past. Explore the ruins of maritime republics that competed with empires. Admire the architectural history, which demonstrates creative flare that has withstood the test of time.

A feast for the senses

The Amalfi Coast is more than a history lesson; it's an immersive sensory experience. Hike along majestic paths, the aroma of wildflowers filling your lungs as you aim for breathtaking vistas. Dive into the cold, refreshing waters of the Mediterranean, with the sun warming your skin as you discover secret coves. Fresh, locally sourced cuisine will treat your taste buds to an explosion of flavor - a genuine foodie's paradise.

Romance at every corner.

The Amalfi Coast emanates romanticism. Intimate piazzas drenched in golden sunshine, romantic meals on balconies overlooking the glittering sea—the ideal environment to make memories that will endure forever. Whether celebrating a honeymoon, an anniversary or just looking for a magical moment with your loved one, the Amalfi Coast will provide a fantastic experience.

Beyond the Picture-Perfect Facade

The Amalfi Coast appeals to everyone. Luxurious hotels give the ultimate pampering experience, but lovely bed and breakfasts provide a more intimate setting. Kayakers may explore secluded coves, while hikers can face complex challenges. Families will discover child-friendly beaches and charming villages with a laid-back ambiance.

This is just a sample of what awaits you on the Amalfi Coast. Whether you want leisure, adventure, cultural immersion, or pure romance, this small piece of heaven offers something for everyone. So pack your bags, embrace your wanderlust, and prepare to find paradise on the Amalfi coast.

Insider Tips from Your Amalfi Coast Guru:

This guide will serve as a road map, but keep in mind that the genuine enchantment of the Amalfi Coast lies in becoming lost in its beauty. Wander into secret alleys, start conversations with people (a few basic Italian words can go a long way!), and enjoy the unexpected moments that make travel so memorable.

Chapter 2: Brief History of the Amalfi Coast

As you stand on the balcony of your quaint Amalfi Coast hotel, staring out at the turquoise waves and pastel-colored cottages clinging to the cliffs, you may wonder how this breathtaking scene came to be. The answer is in a rich tapestry of history woven with commerce, conquest, and creative excellence threads. Let us dig into the exciting history of this seaside paradise.

Early Beginnings: From humble beginnings to a maritime powerhouse

Your journey through time begins in the first century AD. The Amalfi Coast, once known as the Dukedom of Amalfi, was a collection of tiny, generally self-sufficient fishing communities. Life was simple, centered on agriculture and the riches of the sea. However, about the eighth Century, a transition occurred. The Amalfitans became a maritime powerhouse, capitalizing on their strategic position and skillful nautical skills.

A Republic on the Rise: Amalfi's Golden Age

By the ninth Century, the Dukedom of Amalfi had become the Amalfi Republic. This autonomous kingdom existed for centuries, becoming prominent in Mediterranean commerce. They developed trade lines from North Africa to Constantinople, and their knowledge of shipbuilding and navigation was unparalleled. During this golden period, they brought enormous riches and prosperity to the Amalfi Coast.

A Legacy in Stone: The Rise of Architecture and Art.

The Amalfi Republic's riches were not spent only on luxurious lives. They spent extensively in the growth of their towns and cities. Discover this tradition firsthand as you tour Amalfi's spectacular Duomo (Cathedral), a Romanesque architectural marvel. Stroll around the picturesque piazzas and see the complex facades of old buildings, each of which exemplifies the creative energy that thrived throughout this time.

Winds of Change: Challenges and Alliances.

The Amalfi Republic was not impervious to foreign pressures. Pirate raids and rivalry from other maritime powers like Pisa and Genoa eroded their influence. In the eleventh Century, a strategic partnership was formed with the Normans, who supplied military security. However, this union eventually contributed to the demise of the Amalfi Republic. By the 12th Century, the Normans had included Amalfi in their growing realm.

Life Under New Rulers: A Changing Landscape.

Though no longer an autonomous country, the Amalfi Coast remained a vital commercial hub, the Normans, the Hohenstaufen dynasty, and finally, the Angevin monarchs understood the region's strategic value. However, the emphasis switched from marine commerce to agricultural, with lemon production becoming as a significant sector.

A Period of Decline and Renewal: From the 16th Century forward

The 16th Century was a time of deterioration for the Amalfi Coast. Conflicts between European nations and plague outbreaks had a significant impact. To survive, the area shifted its concentration to local agriculture and fishing.

However, a modest comeback occurred in the Eighteenth Century. European artists and authors' rediscovery of the Amalfi Coast's beauty reignited interest in the area. This ultimately led to the advent of tourism in the nineteenth Century, which transformed the Amalfi Coast into the popular holiday destination it is today.

Walk in the Footsteps of History

As you visit the beautiful towns and villages along the Amalfi Coast, remember that you are not only appreciating the magnificent surroundings. You are following in the footsteps of a rich and intriguing past. The Amalfi Coast is infused with history, from the adventurous energy of the Amalfi Republic to the artistic heritage that continues to attract tourists. So keep a look out for historical markers, tour old churches, and let the echoes of the past heighten your appreciation for this genuinely unique part of the globe.

Chapter 3: When To Visit The Amalfi Coast (Weather, Seasons, and Crowds)

The Amalfi Coast entices visitors with its seductive beauty all year round. But with some forethought, you can elevate your vacation from good to genuinely memorable. As your Amalfi Coast expert, I'm here to reveal the secrets of each season, allowing you to plan your holiday at the best moment.

Spring (March-May): A Breath of Fresh Air

Spring fills the Amalfi Coast with a bright hue. The hillsides are covered with wildflowers, the air is filled with the buzz of bees, and the temperature rises to a pleasant level. This shoulder season has various benefits:

- **Smaller crowds:** Compared to peak summer, there will be fewer visitors, enabling you to fully appreciate the beauty of the cities and villages.
- **Pleasant weather:** Avoid the summer heat while enjoying mild days and chilly evenings. This is ideal for hiking or other outdoor activities.
- **Blooming landscapes:** See the Amalfi Coast at its most vivid, with brilliant flowers adding a new dimension of beauty to your images.

- **Lower prices:** Accommodation and travel expenses are often less expensive than during high season.

Insider Tip: Spring is an excellent season for trekking enthusiasts. The trails are less congested, and the wildflowers provide a stunning background for explorations. Pack a light raincoat just in case it rains.

Summer (June-August): A Season of Sun and Celebration

Summer reigns supreme along the Amalfi Coast. The sun casts a golden light over the turquoise waters, making it the perfect season for beachgoers and water lovers. Here's what you may expect:

Perfect beach weather:
- Bask in the warm sun.
- Swim in the crystal-clear Mediterranean.
- Enjoy the lively beach scene.

- **Festivals and events:** Throughout summer, the Amalfi Coast comes alive with exciting festivals and cultural events. Immerse yourself in local customs and festivals.

- **Lively atmosphere:** Expect lively cities and active nightlife. This is an excellent opportunity to watch, dine al fresco, and soak up the festive mood.

- Keep in mind that summer is the busiest tourist season. Prepare for increased crowds, particularly around significant sites. Accommodation and transport expenditures will be at their peak.

Insider Tip: If you want to enjoy the sun but prefer a more relaxed atmosphere, come in early June or September. You'll still enjoy the nice weather, but the crowds will be lower.

Autumn (September to November): A Touch of Tranquility

As summer fades, the Amalfi Coast enters a season of tranquil beauty. Here's what fall has to offer:

- **Pleasant temperatures:** The summer heat has subsided, making touring and exploration more enjoyable.
- **Fewer crowds:** The tourist rush has subsided, resulting in a more calm and intimate ambiance.
- **Harvest season:** Enjoy the delectable abundance of the Amalfi Coast as local markets fill with fresh food such as grapes, lemons, and olives.
- **Vibrant foliage:** Watch the hillsides shift with the changing hues of fall leaves, lending a distinct beauty to the area.

Insider Tip: Autumn is a fantastic season for foodies. Many restaurants provide seasonal menus with fresh, local ingredients. Make sure to taste meals made with locally produced grapes and olives.

Winter (December–February): A Serene Escape

Winter throws a calm spell over the Amalfi Coast. While some companies may have reduced hours, the off-season provides a distinct viewpoint.

- **Tranquility reigns supreme:** Discover cities and villages without high-season crowds.
- **Affordable prices:** Get the most fantastic offers on accommodations and travel.
- **Moderate weather:** Compared to northern Europe, temperatures are mild, making it an ideal winter sun destination.
- **Festive charm:** During the holiday season, visit the Amalfi Coast, which is decked out with Christmas decorations and marketplaces.
- **Things to Remember:** Be prepared for the odd rain shower. Some restaurants and stores may have reduced hours or shut altogether.

Insider Tip: Winter is ideal for budget tourists searching for reasonable prices. Pack an umbrella and some comfortable walking shoes and prepare to see the Amalfi Coast at its most peaceful.

The Final Verdict: Selecting Your Ideal Amalfi Coast Season.

Finally, the ideal time to visit the Amalfi Coast depends on your priorities:
- If you want to enjoy the sun and the bustling nightlife, summer is the time to go.
- Spring and fall provide lovely weather with fewer tourists.
- Winter is an excellent time to travel on a budget and relax.

Whatever season you visit, the Amalfi Coast will fascinate you with its beauty, charm, and rich history. So, pack your luggage!

Part 2: Plan Your Trip

Chapter 4: Getting There and Around (Flights, Ferries, Buses, and Car Rentals)

Congratulations! You have opted to go on an Amalfi Coast excursion. Now comes the fascinating work of organizing your trip and exploring this picturesque wonderland. Fear not, for I, your Amalfi Coast expert, am here to provide the knowledge you need to overcome any transportation difficulty.

Taking Flight: Landing Dreams on the Amalfi Coast

Naples Capodichino International Airport (NAP) is the most popular entrance to the Amalfi Coast. Here's how you go from aircraft to paradise:

Direct Flights: Airlines provide seasonal direct flights from numerous destinations worldwide to Naples. Prices vary based on your origin location and travel dates, but a round-trip ticket should cost between ***€200 and €1000 (US$220 to $1100).***

Connecting Flights: Many passengers prefer connecting flights via major European hubs such as Frankfurt, Paris, and Amsterdam. This may be a less expensive choice, but remember to take in connection delays when comparing pricing.

Pro tip: Book your flights well in advance to get the best rates, particularly during the high season (June–August).

Once You Touch Down: Your Amalfi Coast Transfer Options

Now that you've arrived in Naples, you have numerous options to reach your Amalfi Coast location.

Private Transfer is the most convenient choice, particularly if you're going in a group or with bags. Prices vary from *€150 to €300 (US$165 to $330)*, depending on distance and vehicle size. Pre-booking is advised.

Taxi: Taxi are widely accessible at the airport, but be prepared for high prices, particularly during peak season. Depending on traffic, a journey to Sorrento will cost between *€100 and €200 (US$110 to $220)*.

Train: A low-cost choice, although not the most convenient. The Naples Centrale rail station links to Sorrento (€10-€20, US$11-$22), from whence you can get a bus or boat to your destination.

Explore the Coast: Your Amalfi Coast Transportation Network.

Once you've arrived at your base, here's how to explore the breathtaking Amalfi Coast:

Buses: The SITA bus operator has a robust network that connects all main towns along the coast. Tickets are paid on board and cost between €5 and *€10 (US$5.50-$11)* for each trip. Be prepared for crowds and delays during the busy season.

Ferries provide a picturesque and peaceful method to travel between coastal communities. Ferries run from Salerno, Amalfi, Positano, Sorrento, and Capri. Prices vary according to the route and season, but expect to spend between €15 and €30 (US$16.50 to $33) for each leg.

Car rental provides the greatest freedom, particularly if you want to visit off-the-beaten-path destinations. However, driving around the Amalfi Coast may be difficult owing to small, curving roads and scarce parking. Rental charges begin at about €50 (US$55) per day, including petrol and probable parking fees.

Insider Tip: If you want to visit many museums and sites, consider obtaining a Campania Artecard. This ticket provides free public transit within a defined area for a given period.

The Final Gear Shift: Selecting Your Amalfi Coast Ride

Your vacation style and budget will determine the best mode of transportation.

- **Buses are a practical and cost-effective choice for budget visitors who are okay with crowds.**

- **Ferries provide a gorgeous and soothing experience.**
- **Car rentals are great for experienced drivers who like challenging routes and want the opportunity to discover hidden treasures.**

The Amalfi Coast welcomes you no matter how you get there. So, pack your luggage, pick up your transportation, and prepare to experience the enchantment of this unique place!

Chapter 5: Where to Stay (Choosing an Amalfi Coast Town)

The Amalfi Coast, with its majestic cliffs, pastel-colored villages, and blue waves, has many lovely places to call home throughout your journey. However, selecting the correct one might take a lot of work. Fear not, intrepid traveler! As your Amalfi Coast expert, I'm here to walk you through the alternatives, helping you locate the ideal area to relax and make memorable memories.

Luxury Seekers: How to Live Like a La Dolce Vita Star

If you want extravagance and outstanding service, these sumptuous havens will make you feel like royalty:

Le Sirenuse, Positano (Price Range: €1000+ per night): Situated in the center of Positano, this legendary 5-star hotel offers stunning vistas, infinity pools, and Michelin-starred food. It is ideal for individuals who want the ultimate pampering experience.

Santa Caterina Hotel, Amalfi (Price Range: €700+ per night): This cliffside hotel is steeped in history and elegance. It offers panoramic views, luxury accommodations, and a private beach. It is ideal for a romantic break or a sumptuous retreat.

Palazzo Murat, Positano (Price Range: €500+ per night): This hotel, a renovated 18th-century palace, exudes grandeur with its magnificent decor, private gardens, and breathtaking sea views. It is ideal for people who value a sense of heritage with their luxury.

For the budget-conscious traveler: Stretching Your Euros Further.

The Amalfi Coast does not need to break the bank. Here are some attractive and cheap options:

Hotel La Marinella, Amalfi (prices range from €100 to €200 per night): This family-run hotel has a warm and inviting environment, pleasant accommodations, and spectacular sea views. It is located outside the main town center and offers a calmer and more economical option.

Hostel Beverello, Sorrento (price range: €30-€50 per night): This bustling hostel is an excellent option for social butterflies and budget travelers. It offers dorm and individual rooms, common areas, and scheduled events.

La Locanda del Marinaio, Praiano (Price Range: €150-€200 per night): This quaint bed and breakfast in Praiano provides a more relaxed ambiance than the hustle and bustle of Positano. Enjoy breathtaking ocean views, courteous service, and a great breakfast, which are included in the price.

For the eco-warrior: Staying Green in Paradise.

The Amalfi Coast is becoming more environmentally friendly. Here are some sustainable havens for eco-conscious travelers:

Casa Angelina, Praiano (Price Range: €400+ per night): This exquisite eco-resort is dedicated to sustainable principles. Enjoy fantastic sea views, organic gardens, and locally sourced meals in a gorgeous setting.

Eco-Hotel Charme, Amalfi (Price Range: €200+ per night): This beautiful hotel promotes eco-friendly practices and provides comfortable accommodations with breathtaking views. It is ideal for people who wish to reduce their environmental footprint while maintaining comfort.

Limoneto Li Galli, Capri (Price Range: €300+ per night): Located on the island of Capri, this eco-friendly hideaway has lemon orchards, solar panels, and locally grown food. It is ideal for individuals looking for a deluxe retreat emphasizing sustainability.

Beyond the Big Names: Uncovering Hidden Gems.

The Amalfi Coast has more to offer than its iconic cities. Consider these hidden jewels for a unique and maybe lower-cost experience:

- **Atrani** is a lovely, car-free town tucked between Amalfi and Ravello. Its slower pace of life and breathtaking mountain vistas make it a great place to visit.

- **Furore** is a lovely hamlet famed for its fjord and the spectacular fjord-side restaurant, Il Cavatappi.

- **Minori** is a calmer alternative to Amalfi. It has a magnificent beach, historical monuments, and a relaxing attitude.

The key to unlock your Amalfi Coast paradise

Choosing your Amalfi Coast home base depends on your priorities:

- **A deluxe hotel in Positano or Amalfi offers unrivaled elegance and service.**
- **Hostels in Sorrento and beautiful B&Bs in Praiano provide a low-cost option.**
- **Choose an eco-friendly hotel that adheres to responsible practices for a sustainable stay.**
- **For a one-of-a-kind experience, visit hidden jewels like Atrani, Furore, and Minori.**

The Amalfi Coast provides something for everyone, regardless of their preferences. So, pack your luggage, study your ideal retreat, and prepare to find the magic.

Chapter 6: What to Pack (The Essentials for Your Amalfi Coast Adventure)

The Amalfi Coast is enticed by its majestic cliffs, blue waves, and quaint villages. However, before you start on your Italian vacation, make sure you pack the necessary for a pleasant and memorable experience. As your Amalfi Coast expert, I'm here to walk you through your packing list, ensuring you're ready for everything this mesmerizing coastline throws.

Sun Essentials: Soaking in the Amalfi Sunshine

The Amalfi Coast has a beautiful Mediterranean climate, so pack for sun and warmth. These are the non-negotiables.

- **Swimsuits:** Bring at least two swimsuits to dry between dives in the crystal-clear waters. Consider wearing a cover-up when touring the seaside towns.
- **Sunscreen:** To protect your skin, use a broad-spectrum sunscreen with an SPF of at least 30. Pack a reef-safe choice to reduce environmental impact.
- **Sunglasses:** A decent pair of sunglasses protect your eyes from the harsh sunlight. Choose

- polarized glasses to improve clarity, particularly while looking at the glittering water.
- A wide-brimmed hat protects your face and neck from the sun's rays. Choose a breathable material, such as straw or cotton.

Footwear for Every Adventure: Overcoming Cliffs and Cobblestone Streets

The Amalfi Coast has a varied topography, ranging from stunning cliffside walks to lovely cobblestone towns. Pack shoes that are both comfortable and adaptable.

- **Walking Shoes:** Sturdy shoes with high traction are needed for visiting towns and hiking routes. Choose breathable fabrics to keep your feet cool.
- **Sandals:** Bring comfortable sandals to explore the coastal towns and relax by the pool. Choose a pair with adequate arch support if you want to walk long distances.
- **Shoes:** A decent pair of shoes is a flexible alternative for visiting places, going on day excursions, and adding additional support on rugged terrain.

Clothing for Every Occasion: From Beach Chic to Evening Elegance.

The Amalfi Coast caters to various events, so bring a combination of comfortable and fashionable apparel.

- **Pack lightweight textiles** such as cotton and linen for comfortable daily exploration. Wear loose-fitting clothes to remain cool in warm temperatures.
- **Lightweight cover-ups** help wear over your swimwear when touring seaside towns or eating lunch at a waterfront restaurant.
- **Dressier Options:** Bring a dressier attire to enjoy fine dining or attend nighttime activities. A lightweight sundress or a pair of linen slacks with a lovely top would do.

Additional Essentials: Packing for Unexpected Encounters

Here are some more essentials to guarantee you're ready for anything:

- **Reusable Water Bottle:** Staying hydrated is essential, particularly during hot weather. Pack a reusable water bottle to help reduce plastic waste and save money on bottled water.
- **A quick-drying towel** is ideal for drying off after a swim or a cool plunge in a waterfall.
- Capture the splendor of the Amalfi Coast with a high-quality camera. Remember to have a waterproof case if you intend to shoot images near water.
- **Adaptor:** Bring a travel adaptor compatible with Italian outlets to charge your electrical gadgets.
- **Light Jacket:** Evenings may be chilly, particularly during the shoulder seasons. Pack a

lightweight jacket or sweater for increased comfort.
- **Tiny First-Aid Kit:** Keep a tiny first-aid kit on hand to treat minor scrapes and scratches. Include bandages and pain medications.
- **Personal Toiletries:** Bring your regular toiletries, but remember that sunscreen, aftersun lotion, and insect repellant are especially vital on the Amalfi Coast.

Remember, Less is More: While the Amalfi Coast has limitless activities, don't overpack. Many hotels have washing services, so travel light and choose adaptable items that may be mixed and matched.

Bonus tip: Bring a small bag for day excursions and touring places. This frees your hands from lugging a big bag all day.

By following this packing advice, you'll be well-prepared to explore the Amalfi Coast in elegance and comfort. Now, pack your luggage, gather your necessities, and prepare to experience the charm of this fantastic Italian paradise!

Part 3: Must-See Towns and Villages

Chapter 7: Positano, the Pearl of the Amalfi Coast.

Captivated by the town's magic, John Steinbeck once wrote, "Positano bites deep. It is a dream place that isn't quite real when you are there and becomes beckoningly real after you have left." Get ready to be bitten by the Positano bug because this captivating town on the Amalfi Coast is unlike any other.

A Labyrinth of Enchantment: Walking Through Positano's Streets

Labyrinth of Enchantment

Step off the main road and immerse yourself in the heart of Positano. Narrow, pedestrian-only streets dotted with brightly colored residences appear before you. Bougainvillea pours over balconies, providing vibrant color to the environment. Every turn unveils a new treasure, whether a beautiful store selling local crafts, a quiet trattoria smelling of fresh herbs, or a secret piazza brimming with activity. Wander at your own speed, taking in this charming town's sights, sounds, and vitality.

Beaches Calling: Sun, Sand, and Serenity

Beaches beckon

Positano has more than just a cliffside appeal; it also has magnificent beaches where you can soak up the sun. Marina Grande, the principal beach, has a bustling atmosphere. Rent a sun lounger, get a cool drink from a local bar, and bask in the warm Mediterranean sun. Water sports rentals are offered for those who want to experience the shoreline from a fresh viewpoint.

A Secluded Paradise: Exploring Spiaggia dei Conigli

Secluded paradise.

Spiaggia dei Conigli (Rabbit Beach) offers a more isolated experience. This secret cove is only accessible by boat and provides a peaceful sanctuary. The pristine white beach meets turquoise waves to create a picture-perfect landscape. Relax on the beach, take a refreshing plunge, and enjoy being away from the crowd.

A Culinary Adventure Awaits: Tasting the Flavors of Positano

Fresh seafood.

Fresh fish dominate Positano's gastronomic scene. As you go throughout town, odors of garlic, herbs, and freshly baked bread will entice your taste senses. Indulge in flavorful pasta meals such as spaghetti alle vongole (clams) and linguine al limone. Enjoy the day's catch, grilled or served in a classic Zuppa di pesce (fish soup).

Remember to treat your taste buds to aromatic lemon-infused delights, a remarkable monument to the area's citrus richness. Finish your dinner with a scoop of gelato, the ideal way to cool down on a hot day while experiencing the flavors of Italy on a spoon.

A breathtaking panorama: Hiking the Path of the Gods.

Hiking the Path of Gods

Every trip to Positano is complete with beautiful views from above. Lace up your hiking boots and start on a tour down the Path of the Gods (Sentiero degli Dei), a renowned route that connects Positano and Nocelle. The modest trek culminates in breathtaking panoramic views of the Amalfi Coast. Dramatic cliffs drop toward the blue seas below, while colorful settlements hang dangerously to the slopes. The Amalfi Coast's magnificence unfolds in all its majesty, leaving you with an unforgettable memory.

Exploring Beyond Positano: Discovering the Amalfi Coast.

Positano is a compelling location in and of itself, but it also serves as an excellent starting point for exploring the Amalfi Coast. Join a boat cruise to explore secluded coves only accessible by water. Visit the adjacent towns of Amalfi, which has a majestic church, and Sorrento, which is noted for its picturesque streets and rich history. Take a day excursion to Capri and Ischia islands, which offer distinct experiences and stunning landscapes. The Amalfi Coast is your oyster, ready to be explored.

Positano's unmistakable appeal stems from its flawless integration of spectacular beauty, rich history, and lively culture. Whether you want to relax on the beach, see ancient places, or go on a gourmet adventure, Positano has an experience that will last a lifetime.

Chapter 8: Amalfi: History and Culture in a Picturesque Setting.

Amalfi, a name linked with beauty and history, emerges along the Amalfi Coast's majestic cliffs. Brilliant buildings hang dangerously to the hills, their multicolored façade mirroring the Mediterranean's blue waves below. But Amalfi's allure extends well beyond its idyllic surroundings. This old town has a unique history, a lively culture, and an enticing energy that continues to captivate tourists.

A Legacy Etched in Stone: A Journey Through Amalfi's History.

The history of Amalfi dates back centuries. Founded by Romans seeking safety from barbarian assaults, the town quickly developed into a maritime powerhouse. During the Middle Ages, it grew into a significant trade metropolis, rivaling Venice and Genoa. Evidence of this beautiful history may still be found today. The stately **Duomo (Cathedral)**, a UNESCO World Heritage Site, is a marvel of Romanesque architecture, with its soaring façade and delicate mosaics telling stories of Amalfi's golden period. The Cloister of Paradise, a calm refuge inside the cathedral complex, takes visitors back in time with its tranquil gardens and majestic columns.

A Tapestry of Culture: Revealing the Soul of Amalfi

Amalfi's cultural tapestry is woven with strands of heritage, art, and zeal for life. Wander through the small alleyways, and you'll come across secret piazzas filled with inhabitants speaking animatedly. Visit the ***Museo Arsenale Amalfi***, a former shipyard turned museum, to learn about the town's nautical legacy. Watch the magic happen in the nights as the ***Piazza del Duomo*** changes into a colorful stage for street performers and musicians, filling the air with song and laughter.

A Feast for the Senses: Experiencing Amalfi's Culinary Delights

Amalfi's culinary culture celebrates fresh, locally sourced products and time-honored traditions. Enjoy the flavors of the sea with excellent seafood meals such as ***spaghetti alle vongole (clams)*** or a tasty ***Zuppa di pesce (fish soup)***. Indulge in aromatic lemon dishes, which showcase the region's citrus wealth. Enjoy ***sfogliatella***, a flaky pastry filled with ricotta cheese and candied orange peel, a local delicacy that will delight your taste buds.

Beyond the Town Walls: Exploring the Environment of Amalfi

While Amalfi is a beautiful location on its right, it also acts as a jumping-off point for further excursions around the Amalfi Coast. Take a boat cruise and explore secluded coves only accessible by water. Hike the Path of the Gods *(Sentiero degli Dei)*, a renowned trek with stunning panoramic vistas. Explore nearby villages such as *Positano*, noted for its cascading buildings, and *Ravello*, known for its breathtaking gardens and cliffside mansions.

Amalfi is more than simply an attractive face. It's where ancient stones whisper history, culture comes alive in the everyday rhythm of living, and the natural world's beauty inspires wonder. So come and immerse yourself in the charm of Amalfi. Explore its rich history and culture, experience its excellent food, and make unforgettable memories.

Chapter 9: Ravello: Hilltop Paradise with Stunning Views.

Imagine yourself poised high above the Amalfi Coast, staring out over a beautiful view of blue waves, towering cliffs, and quaint hamlet nestled in the hillsides. This is Ravello, a hilltop oasis with breathtaking beauty, history, and cultural riches.

Journey Through Time: Exploring Ravello's Historic Heart

The Grand Duomo (Cathedral)

Wander around Ravello's historic center and take a step back in time. The enormous Duomo (Cathedral), a

beautiful specimen of Romanesque architecture, reminds us of the town's previous splendor. The exterior is adorned with intricate mosaics, while the interiors have paintings and sculptures depicting Ravello's rich history. Explore the intriguing *Villa Rufolo*, a former private mansion turned museum with breathtaking coastline views. Wander around its gorgeous grounds with sculptures and fountains, and envision the opulent festivities here centuries ago.

A feast for the senses: indulging in Ravello's artistic delights.

Ravello's creative significance goes beyond its building. The town has traditionally been a sanctuary for artists and musicians, and its cultural life remains vibrant. Immerse yourself in the opera world at the legendary Wagner Festival, performed yearly in an open-air theater with a beautiful view. Stroll through art galleries displaying the works of local artists or watch a concert in a medieval church, the music reverberating through the old stone walls.

Ravello's tranquil gardens are a haven for relaxation.

Ravello provides a welcome respite from the rush and bustle of the seashore below. Seek tranquillity in the magnificent grounds of *Villa Cimbrone*, a charming sanctuary set in the hills. Wander through groomed lawns covered with brilliant flowers, get lost in the labyrinth of hedges, and enjoy stunning seaside views. The serene environment and soft sounds of nature will leave you feeling refreshed and energized.

A culinary adventure awaits: savoring the flavors of Ravello.

Ravello's food scene celebrates fresh, locally sourced ingredients and traditional dishes. Indulge in delicious pasta dishes such as ravioli loaded with ricotta cheese and spinach, or taste a tasty pizza cooked in a wood-fired oven. Try local delicacies such as *"scialatielli,"* a thick pasta made with local flour and often served with a seafood sauce. Remember to finish your dinner with a piece of *Delizia al limone*, a light and delightful lemon cake that perfectly captures the flavors of the Amalfi Coast.

Beyond the Town Walls: Exploring Ravello's Environs.

While Ravello is a beautiful destination in its own right, it also serves as an excellent starting point for exploring the rest of the Amalfi Coast. Take a picturesque bus journey down to Amalfi, an ancient marine town, or visit the lovely villages of *Atrani and Minori,* each with their distinct personality. For a touch of luxury, take a boat cruise to explore secret coves only accessible by water.

Ravello is more than simply a picturesque village; it's an experience. It's a location where history and culture coexist with stunning natural beauty. Explore its historic core, immerse yourself in its artistic heritage, relax in its quiet gardens, and sample its excellent food. Ravello awaits, eager to make experiences that will last a lifetime.

Chapter 10: Sorrento, a lively gateway to the Amalfi Coast.

"Sorrento is a dream place that isn't quite real when you are there and becomes beckoningly real after you have left." - Steinbeck, John.

This remark truly expresses the character of Sorrento, a thriving town perched on the cliffs above the Bay of Naples. It serves as a vibrant entryway to the Amalfi Coast while maintaining its distinct charm that draws tourists year after year.

A Tapestry Woven Through Time: Revealing Sorrento's Rich History

Sorrento has a rich history.

Sorrento's story dates back millennia. The Greeks founded it in the eighth Century BC, and it has since been a prized possession of successive rulers. Wandering the lovely alleys now reveals remnants of this rich history. The historic center is a treasure trove of historical ruins, including the remains of a Roman temple and a medieval church. Explore the ***Museo Correale,*** a fascinating museum with archeological items, paintings, and sculptures that bring Sorrento's past to life.

A Buzzing Heart: Immerse Yourself in Sorrento's Lively Atmosphere

Sorrento is a vibrant town. Stroll around the lively Piazza Tasso, the central core, and take in the vivid atmosphere. Street performers delight the masses, cafés pour into the cobblestone streets, and the air is full of laughter and conversations. The town becomes a platform for singers and artists in the evenings, providing a delicious taste of Italian nightlife.

A Culinary Paradise: Going on a Gastronomic Adventure

Sorrento is a foodie's paradise, serving a delectable combination of fresh, local ingredients and classic dishes. Indulge in the famous spaghetti alle vongole (clams), a meal that wonderfully reflects the wealth of the adjacent sea. Try the local delicacy, gnocchi alla Sorrentino, a sort of potato gnocchi tossed in a rich tomato sauce with mozzarella cheese. Remember to save space for dessert;

Sorrento is known for its delicious lemons, and a piece of lemon cake or a scoop of lemon gelato is the ideal way to finish your dinner.

Beyond the Town Walls: Exploring the Environment of Sorrento

While Sorrento is a remarkable destination in its own right, it also provides an excellent starting point for exploring the surrounding region. Take a day trip to the stunning Amalfi Coast, which has towering cliffs and beautiful communities such as Positano and Amalfi. Visit the remains of Pompeii, an ancient Roman city trapped in time by volcanic ash, or marvel at the majesty of Mount Vesuvius. This famous volcano continues to captivate travelers.

A Perfect Blend: Sorrento's Enduring Allure.

Sorrento's appeal stems from its ideal combination of history, culture, and natural beauty. Whether you want to explore ancient ruins, immerse yourself in a bustling environment, or eat excellent cuisine, Sorrento offers something for everyone. So come and see why Sorrento is more than simply a gateway to the Amalfi Coast; it's also a fantastic destination in and of itself.

Chapter 11: Hidden Gems: Exploring Smaller Towns (Praiano, Furore, and Atrani

The Amalfi Coast, with legendary cities like Positano and Sorrento, attracts visitors seeking magnificent beauty and vitality. But travel beyond the staples and discover a universe of hidden jewels. Prepare to visit lovely towns with distinct personalities and narratives, providing an authentic taste of Amalfi Coast life.

Praiano: A Relaxing Escape

Praiano

As John Steinbeck famously said, "It is a whole new world, physically and spiritually." That's precisely how you could feel when you arrive at Praiano. Nestled between Positano and Amalfi, this peaceful town provides a nice respite from the noise and bustle of its more renowned neighbors. Pastel-colored buildings slide down cliffsides, their balconies bursting with colorful flowers. Narrow, car-free lanes with local stores invite you to explore while freshly baked bread and cooking sauces permeate the atmosphere.

Seek Serenity: Praiano's appeal stems from its relaxed setting. Relax on the beach, soak up the warm Mediterranean sun, and enjoy a refreshing plunge in the crystal-clear sea. For the more daring, discover secluded coves accessible only by boat, or take a picturesque trek along the coast, which will reward you with spectacular panoramic views.

Indulge Your Inner Foodie: Praiano has many family-run eateries, each serving traditional Amalfi Coast food. Enjoy fresh seafood meals produced with local ingredients, or indulge in handmade pasta combinations that will entice your taste buds. Don't miss out on trying the local delicacy, "scialatielli," a thick pasta dish often served with seafood sauce.

A Perfect Base for Exploration: While Praiano provides a calm getaway, it is also an excellent starting point for exploring the Amalfi Coast. Take a local bus to explore the surrounding villages of Positano and Amalfi, or take a boat cruise to discover secluded coves only accessible by sea.

Praiano is a hidden treasure waiting to be uncovered. It is a place to relax, reconnect with nature, and enjoy the simple joys of Italian living.

Furor: When Nature and Art Collide

Furore

Prepare to be amazed when you visit Furore, a lovely town on the Amalfi Coast. This site is famous for its spectacular fjord, a deep valley cut by a flowing waterfall.

Take an exciting journey down the fjord in a traditional wooden boat for an unforgettable local experience.

Furore's creative energy is shown in its various galleries, which display the works of local artists. Stroll through the small lanes to see hidden jewels like the Conca dei Marini, an open-air museum with sculptures tucked in the rocks. Watch the magic happen in the nights as the fjord changes into a stage for concerts and shows, the music reverberating down the canyon.

A Culinary Adventure Awaits: Furore has a fantastic assortment of restaurants, many with terraces facing the fjord, offering a stunning background for your lunch. Indulge in fresh seafood dishes, a warm plate of pasta, or a piece of wood-fired pizza. Remember to sample the local limoncello, a delightful lemon liqueur that wonderfully embodies the flavor of the Amalfi Coast.

Furore is an excellent choice for a day excursion from surrounding towns such as Praiano or Positano. Explore its distinctive attractions, immerse yourself in its creative environment, and have a tasty dinner while admiring the spectacular vista.

Atrani - A Fairytale Escape

Atrani

As you explore Atrani, a car-free town on the Amalfi Coast, step back in time. This lovely village, known as "the pearl of the Amalfi Coast," has a timeless beauty with its colorful buildings arranged around a central square. Wander through the small, cobblestone alleyways, past historic churches and quaint stores, and enjoy the tranquil environment.

Atrani provides a peek into the traditional Amalfi Coast way of life. Mix with pleasant people, observe artists making traditional items, and appreciate the slower pace of life. In the evenings, meet at the busy plaza to enjoy a gelato while listening to the lovely sounds of conversation and laughter filling the air.

Explore Hidden Gems: Beyond the Main.

Square, Atrani has hidden jewels waiting to be unearthed. Climb the steep staircase to the Santa Maria Maddalena church, a stunning example of Romanesque architecture, and see the beautiful murals and spectacular vistas. For a sense of adventure, visit the remains of the medieval watchtower, which provides panoramic views of the coastline.

Atrani is a culinary paradise with a fantastic range of family-run eateries, many of which have terraces that overlook the sea. Enjoy fresh fish meals harvested only hours before, flavorful handmade pasta masterpieces, or try the local delicacy, "scarcella," a sweet bread stuffed with ricotta and candied fruit.

A Perfect Base for Relaxation: While Atrani provides a peaceful retreat, it is also perfectly positioned for visiting the Amalfi Coast. Take a lovely stroll along the coast to nearby Amalfi, or take a local bus to the lively town of Sorrento.

Atrani is a hidden treasure that embodies the spirit of the Amalfi Coast. It's a place to calm down, enjoy the simple joys of Italian living, and make memories that last a lifetime.

So, go beyond the typical Amalfi Coast attractions. Explore the lovely towns of Praiano, Furore, and Atrani, each with its distinct character and tale to tell. Discover secret coves, learn about local customs, and enjoy beautiful meals while admiring the stunning vistas. The Amalfi Coast's hidden beauties are waiting to surprise and thrill you.

Part 4: Activities and Experiences.

Chapter 12: Hiking the Amalfi Coast: Stunning Trails and Panoramic Views

"The Amalfi Coast is more than just a beautiful place; it's a place that makes you feel like you're in a movie."

This is a fitting statement, particularly given the spectacular paths that snake around the towering cliffs, providing panoramic vistas right out of a dream. Hiking the Amalfi Coast is a thrilling experience that mixes physical hardship with breathtaking scenery.

A Journey Through Nature's Masterpiece

Sentiero degli Dei

The Amalfi Coast has a network of well-kept paths suitable for all ability levels. One of the most famous walks is the Path of the Gods (Sentiero degli Dei), a moderate path that connects Positano and Nocelle. As you weave down the cliffside, the turquoise waters of the Mediterranean Sea appear below, sprinkled with lovely settlements perched perilously on the slopes. The sheer cliffs and dense greenery provide a beautiful landscape, making every step a picture-perfect moment.

Beyond the Main Event: Although the Path of the Gods is a must-do for every Amalfi Coast hiker, there are plenty of additional routes to discover. The Valley of the Mills (Valle delle Ferriere) is a challenging but enjoyable climb through a green valley with antique mills and waterfalls. Consider taking a shorter but equally picturesque trek from Amalfi to Atrani, a small town along the coast.

Hiking the Amalfi Coast is more than simply a physical challenge; it is also a sensual experience. The fresh Mediterranean air energizes your lungs, the aroma of wildflowers perfumes the air, and the sound of crashing waves gives a natural soundtrack to your adventure. When you reach the top of each climb, you will be rewarded with spectacular panoramic views that will take your breath away.

Planning Your Hike: Plan and prepare before beginning your Amalfi Coast trip. Choose a path appropriate for your fitness level and expertise, wear durable shoes with adequate traction, and pack enough drink and sunscreen.

The trails may become crowded, particularly during peak season, so plan your trip early in the morning. Many municipalities provide maps and guides to help you navigate the paths.

Hiking the Amalfi Coast is more than simply physical exercise; it's an opportunity to reconnect with nature, see the region's beauty from a new viewpoint, and immerse yourself in local culture. You could encounter friendly villagers tending to their olive trees, stumble across secret beaches accessible only by foot, or find old remains buried among the hills.

So, lace up your hiking boots and get ready to be astounded. The Amalfi Coast welcomes you with its network of beautiful pathways, delivering an extraordinary trip that mixes physical challenge and unmatched beauty. Let the majestic cliffs and breathtaking landscapes of the Amalfi Coast serve as the setting for a memorable Italian experience.

Chapter 13: Beach Activities: Sunbathing, Swimming, and Water Sports.

"The Amalfi Coast is a symphony of senses: the smell of lemon trees, the sound of crashing waves, the warmth of the sun on your skin." –

Prepare to be immersed in this symphony as you visit the Amalfi Coast's beaches. Here, immaculate expanses of beach and brilliant blue seas invite you to soak up the sun, take refreshing dives, and discover the marvels of the undersea world.

Sunbathing Bliss: Find Your Perfect Spot

Sunbathing bliss.

The Amalfi Coast has various beaches to suit everyone's tastes. Marina Grande Beach in Positano offers a typical sunbathing experience. Rent a comfy sun lounger, have a refreshing drink from a neighboring bar, and relax beneath the warm Mediterranean sun. Colorful cottages sliding down the cliffside offer a lovely background, while the soft sound of lapping waves produces a relaxing environment.

Secluded Paradise: Uncovering Hidden Coves

If you want a more isolated experience, go beyond the famous beaches. Many isolated coves, only accessible by boat, provide a refuge of peace. Spiaggia dei Conigli (Rabbit Beach) in Positano is a popular destination, with immaculate white sand and crystal-clear seas perfect for swimming and snorkeling. Marina del Cantone in Nerano provides a breathtaking landscape and a laid-back environment, ideal for escaping the crowd.

A Refreshing Dip: Cooling Down in the Mediterranean

The Amalfi Coast's blue waves are just too alluring to refuse. Dive into the refreshing Mediterranean and feel the cool embrace of the water. The beach provides limitless options, whether you prefer a leisurely paddle or a challenging swim. The more daring may explore the aquatic world with a snorkeling or scuba diving adventure. Underwater, vibrant coral reefs and a broad range of marine creatures await discovery.

Water Sports Paradise: Embracing the Adventure.

The Amalfi Coast is a haven for water sports fans. For those looking for thrills, try jet skiing or parasailing and experience the exhilaration as you zoom over the sea. Kayaking and paddleboarding provide a more relaxing approach to exploring the coastline, enabling you to find secret coves and take in stunning vistas from a different viewpoint.

Beyond the Beach: Activities for All Interests

The Amalfi Coast offers more than simply sun, beach, and sea. Many seaside communities have boat cruises, which enable you to see the shore from a fresh viewpoint. Discover secret caves, isolated coves, and majestic cliffs only accessible by boat. For those looking to taste history, see the remains of old Roman villas tucked along the shore, relics of a past period.

So bring your swimwear, sunscreen, and spirit of exploration. The beaches of the Amalfi Coast beckon, providing an ideal balance of leisure, amusement, and discovery. Whether you want a traditional sunbathing experience, a soothing plunge in the crystal-clear seas, or an adrenaline-pumping water activity, the Amalfi Coast offers something for everyone. Allow the symphony of the Amalfi Coast's senses to wash over you, leaving you with unforgettable recollections.

Chapter 14: Boating Adventures: Exploring the Coastline at Sea

The Amalfi Coast, with its majestic cliffs, quaint towns, and secret bays, reveals its natural glory from the sea. Taking a boat trip is an exciting experience that provides a new perspective on the coastline's magnificent vistas and hidden gems.

A Journey Through Time: Coastline Gems Unveiled.

As you start sailing, the renowned villages of the Amalfi Coast emerge in all their beauty. Positano, with its pastel-colored villas tumbling down the cliffs, seems like something from a fantasy. Amalfi, the old marine town, has a stunning church and a picturesque port. Smaller settlements, such as Atrani and Praiano, ensconced in beautiful foliage, provide a peek into a more traditional way of life.

Beyond the Main Stage: Finding Hidden Gems.

A boat cruise's genuine thrill consists of exploring beyond the major sites. Expert captains will guide you to secret coves accessible only by sea. Discover isolated beaches with immaculate sand and clean seas ideal for swimming and snorkeling. Explore breathtaking sea caverns such as the green Grotto (Grotta dello Smeraldo), where sunlight penetrates through the water, creating a stunning green hue.

A Glimpse of History: Unveiling Ancient Ruins

The Amalfi Coast's history is inextricably interwoven with the water. Boat trips often pass past the remains of old Roman villas on cliffs, relics of a bygone age. Consider the life of individuals who formerly lived in these magnificent homes, enjoying stunning vistas and a pleasant Mediterranean wind.

A Feast for the Senses: Enjoying the Amalfi Coast Experience

A boat cruise around the Amalfi Coast is a sensory feast. The salty sea air energizes your lungs, waves breaking against the cliffs provide a natural soundtrack, and the stunning view unfolds in front of you like a painting. Many excursions allow swimming in hidden coves or snorkeling in bright coral reefs filled with marine life.

Beyond the boat: Exploring farther

Boat cruises may serve as a starting point for further exploration. Disembark in quaint towns and stroll along tiny alleyways adorned with colorful buildings and local stores. Enjoy a fantastic seafood meal on a waterfront deck with fresh, local foods and spectacular views. For adventure, stroll along magnificent routes that weave through the hills, providing panoramic coastline views.

Choosing Your Boat Tour Adventure.

The Amalfi Coast provides various boat cruises to suit different interests and budgets. Group cruises on bigger boats are a friendly and cheap alternative, while private boat tours are more intimate and personalized. Many excursions offer extra activities such as swimming, snorkeling, and visiting secret caves.

A Journey to Remember: Making Lasting Memories.

A boat cruise around the Amalfi Coast is more than simply a sightseeing trip; it's a memorable experience. It's an opportunity to disengage from the daily grind, reconnect with nature, and make memories that will last a lifetime. So, take sail and go on an exploration journey to uncover the Amalfi Coast's hidden mysteries.

Chapter 15: Cultural Highlights: Museums, Churches, and Historic Sites

The Amalfi Coast is more than simply a destination for sunbathers and beachgoers; it is rich in history and culture. Beyond the stunning cliffs and lovely towns lies a treasure of a wealth of museums, cathedrals, and historical monuments waiting to be discovered. Prepare to embark on a riveting trip through time, with each turn revealing a fascinating narrative from the Amalfi Coast's rich history.

A Glance at Maritime Glory: The Museo Arsenale Amalfi.

Museo Arsenale Amalfi

The Museo Arsenale Amalfi explores the Amalfi Coast's marine past. This exciting museum in a historic shipyard dating back to the seventh Century commemorates the region's long and distinguished past as a significant maritime force. Explore interactive exhibitions with ship models, navigation gear, and historical maps, each telling a story of daring expeditions and remarkable discoveries.

The Amalfi Duomo is a masterpiece in stone.

The Cathedral of Amalfi

No visit to Amalfi is complete without seeing the magnificent **Duomo (Cathedral).** This beautiful specimen of Romanesque architecture designated a UNESCO World Heritage Site, reminds the town of its previous greatness. Step inside to see the high ceilings, stunning mosaics of biblical figures, and shining marble flooring. The nearby Cloister of Paradise provides a tranquil refuge, with quiet gardens and historic columns that take you back in time.

A Hidden Gem: The Museo Correale in Sorrento.

Museo Correale in Sorrento

Visit Sorrento and experience the intriguing Museo Correale. This museum, housed in a stunning 18th-century palace, exhibits a vast collection of items that illustrate the narrative of the Sorrento Peninsula. Admire ancient Roman statues, peruse Renaissance painting collections, and marvel at the wonderful majolica pottery that symbolizes the region's creative past. Temporary displays highlight the works of current artists, ensuring there is always something new to explore.

A Tapestry of Faith: Exploring the Amalfi Coast's Churches

The Amalfi Coast is dotted with lovely churches, each with its architectural style and cultural riches. The Chiesa di Santa Maria Assunta in Positano has a beautiful majolica dome, while the Chiesa di San Giorgio in Ravello combines Romanesque and Byzantine elements. Step into these hallowed rooms and take up the serene ambiance filled with paintings, sculptures, and religious relics.

A Window into the Past: Unearthing Roman Ruins

History lovers will enjoy visiting the relics of old Roman villages along the Amalfi Coast. The remains of a Roman villa at Conca dei Marini provide insight into the lifestyle of wealthy Romans who once had beautiful views of the shore. In Ravello, the archaeological site of Cimbrone exhibits the ruins of a Roman villa rustica, a functioning farm that flourished centuries ago.

Beyond The Walls: A Cultural Tapestry

Museums and historical buildings are not the only cultural attractions on the Amalfi Coast. Throughout the year, attractive communities offer lively festivals that honor local customs and creative expressions. Witness the enthralling procession at the Feast of San Gennaro in Naples, or be captivated by the famed Wagner Festival in Ravello's open-air theater. In the evenings, visit local galleries presenting brilliant artists' works or attend a concert in a medieval church to immerse yourself in the region's colorful cultural tapestry.

A journey of discovery:

Exploring the Amalfi Coast's cultural pleasures is a voyage of discovery. Each museum, church, and historical landmark reveals a fascinating episode from the region's rich history. So, listen to the tales recounted by ancient stones, appreciate creative marvels, and get immersed in the complex cultural tapestry that defines the Amalfi Coast. Your artistic journey awaits.

Chapter 16: Foodie Paradise: Amalfi Coast Cuisine and Cooking Classes.

The Amalfi Coast is more than just a visual feast; it is also a sensory feast, and your taste buds will be in for a treat. Fresh, local products, traditional recipes handed down through generations, and magnificent scenery combine to create a gastronomic paradise. Prepare to go on a gastronomic adventure, enjoying the essence of the Amalfi Coast on your plate and learning how to reproduce these delicacies yourself.

A celebration of freshness: local flavors take center stage.

Amalfi Coast food is a symphony of fresh, seasonal ingredients. Shellfish harvested directly from the crystal-clear seas is prominent, with meals such as **spaghetti alle vongole (clams) and fritters mista (assorted fried shellfish)** exciting the taste senses. Locally produced veggies such as **zucchini, eggplant, and tomatoes are tasteful,** while aromatic lemons give a refreshing touch to many recipes. Please don't overlook the region's olive oil, a golden elixir derived from centuries-old olive orchards that imparts a deep depth of flavor to everything it touches.

Indulge Your Inner Foodie by Exploring Renowned Restaurants

The Amalfi Coast has a broad array of eateries, each with its distinct interpretation of classic Amalfi Coast food. For an outstanding fine dining experience, visit **La Sponda at Hotel Le Sirenuse in Positano.** This Michelin-starred restaurant offers spectacular views of the sea and inventive meals made with the best ingredients from the area. **La Cucina di Mamma Agata in Ravello** provides a more relaxed but superb dining experience. This family-run establishment delivers traditional home-cooked meals, including pasta specialties like ravioli packed with ricotta cheese and spinach that leave you wanting more.

Discover the Secrets: Unveiling Cooking Classes

Do you want to take a bit of Amalfi Coast home with you? Numerous culinary lessons allow you to discover the secrets of traditional Amalfi Coast food from local cooks. Imagine yourself in a gorgeous kitchen, surrounded by rolling hills and magnificent vistas, learning to cook fresh pasta from scratch, create a tasty sauce, and master the art of tiramisu. Many workshops end with a fantastic lunch, enabling you to enjoy your handiwork while socializing with fellow foodies. Consider La Cucina del Nonno in Positano, a well-known culinary school that provides hands-on courses in a picturesque location.

Beyond the Plate: Culinary Adventure Awaits

The Amalfi Coast's gastronomic journey goes beyond restaurants and cooking lessons. Explore local markets with fresh fruit, vibrant spices, and aromatic cheeses. Local delicacies include "scialatielli," a thick pasta dish often served with a seafood sauce, and "delizia al limone," a light and refreshing lemon cake. In the evenings, join a wine-tasting session to learn about the region's distinctive wines, which pair nicely with the local food.

A journey for your taste buds.

The Amalfi Coast is a gastronomic heaven waiting to be discovered. From indulging in fresh seafood delicacies at famous restaurants to discovering the secrets of ancient recipes in a cooking class, your taste senses will be taken on an incredible trip. So come hungry, enjoy the local cuisines, and make gastronomic memories that last a lifetime.

Part 5: Practical Information.

Chapter 17: Budgeting Your Trip (Costs, Transportation, and Accommodation)

The Amalfi Coast entices visitors with its stunning cliffs, picturesque towns, and turquoise seas, but it is also recognized as a wealthy getaway. However, with proper preparation and budgeting, you may enjoy the Amalfi Coast's allure without breaking the bank. Here's an overview of the main expenses to consider.

Transportation:

- **Flights:** Prices vary widely based on your departure location, season, and airline. Consider flying into Naples International Airport (NAP) for the most flexibility. The shoulder seasons (spring and autumn) frequently provide excellent flight rates.

- **Ferry:** Ferries link the main towns on the Amalfi Coast. Although handy, they may add up. If you travel often, consider obtaining a multi-day pass.

- **Bus:** Buses are a more cost-effective way to commute between towns. While slower than ferries, they provide a lovely route along the shore.

- **Private transportation:** For a more premium experience, try reserving private transportation between airports, rail stations, and your hotel.

Accommodation:

- **Hotels:** The Amalfi Coast offers diverse accommodations, from luxurious homes on cliffs to family-run guesthouses. Prices vary widely according to location, amenities, and season. For a more economical choice, consider vacationing in tiny communities outside of the major tourist areas.

- **AirBnB/Vacation Rentals:** Renting an apartment or villa provides excellent room and flexibility, particularly for families and groups. To save money on meals, look for choices that offer self-catering amenities.

- **Hostels:** Hostels are an affordable choice for lone travelers. They provide a social environment and dorm beds for a fraction of the cost of a hotel room.

General costs:

- **Food:** Dining out may be pricey, particularly in famous tourist destinations. Consider budgeting for a combination of restaurant meals and self-prepared breakfasts and lunches. Look for eateries that provide fixed-price menus or "piano" (worker's lunch) as a cheaper choice.

- **Activities:** Boat trips, culinary lessons, and museum and historical site admission fees may increase. Prioritize the most essential activities for you and look into free or low-cost choices such as hiking trails and beautiful overlooks.

- **Mementos:** Unique, handmade mementos are appealing, but make a budget and adhere to it. Consider buying modest, locally crafted goods as souvenirs.

Savings Tips:

- **Travel during the shoulder seasons:** The shoulder seasons (spring and autumn) provide beautiful weather, fewer people, and typically reduced pricing on flights and accommodations.

- **Consider a Package Deal:** Many travel businesses provide packages that include flights and accommodations, sometimes at a reduced cost.

- **Purchase a Campania Arte card:** This card provides free or reduced admission to museums, archeological sites, and public transportation across Campania, including the Amalfi Coast.

- **Walk or use public transportation:** Although handy, cabs may be pricey. Consider walking between adjacent towns or using the public bus for a low-cost exploration method.

- **Pack Lightly:** Many hotels charge extra for baggage storage. Pack little to avoid luggage costs on cheap flights.

If you properly organize your transportation, lodging, and activities, you can enjoy the enchantment of the Amalfi Coast without breaking the budget. Remember that the most significant experiences on the Amalfi Coast are frequently free: taking in the stunning vistas, discovering quaint towns, and eating fresh, local cuisine. So, establish a reasonable budget, pick your must-dos, and prepare to make beautiful memories with this Italian treasure.

Chapter 18: Language and Communication (Essential Italian Phrases).

Its spectacular views and colorful culture entice the Amalfi Coast, but learning a new language may be frightening. Fear not, intrepid traveler! With a few key Italian words and a little confidence, you'll speak with locals and charm through your Amalfi Coast experience. Here's a crash course in conversational Italian that will make you feel comfortable and understood:

Greetings and pleasantries:

- **Good morning (boo-on-jor-no).** Good morning (till lunch).
- **Buona sera (boo-na seh-rah):** Good evening.
- **Hello (chow):** Hello/goodbye (informal)
- **Salve (pronounced "sahl-veh"):** Hello (formal).
- **Thanks (grah-tsee-eh):** Thank you!
- **Prego (pronounced: pre-go)** You're welcome (also means "please").
- **Scusi (pronounced sku-see):** Excuse me.
- **I apologize (mee scu-see).** Excuse me (be more nice).
- **Per favore (fah-voh-reh):** Please

Essential questions:

- **Do you speak English? (Par-la Een-gleh-seh)** Do you speak English?
- **Non-Capisco (non-Kah-pee-sko):** I do not comprehend.
- **How much does it cost? (Kwahn-Toh Coh-sta)** How much does it cost?
- **Where are they...? (Doh-veh, see Tro-va...)** Where are...?
- **Can I have...? (Poh-sso Ah-veh-reh...)** Can I have...?
- **Please provide the following account:** The bill.

Dining delights:

- **Good appetite (bwon appeh-tee-toh).** Enjoy your food!
- **Mi piacerebbe.** I would prefer...
- **A glass of wine (pronounced "bik-ee-eh-reh dee vee-no").** A glass of wine.
- **Acqua (pronounced ah-kwa) Water:** Birra (pronounced bee-rah). Beer Caffè (pronounced cash-feh): Coffee
- Navigating the coast
- **Where can I catch the bus? (Doh-veh Poh-sso Pren-deh-reh L'ow-to-boos)** Where do I catch the bus?
- **I need a cab, please.** I'd want a cab, please.
- **How much time do we need? (Kwan-toh tempo chee vo-leh)** How long will this take?

- **Mi fermo qui (mee fer-mo kwee).** I will get off here.

Beyond the basics:

- Bella (bel-la) means beautiful (feminine).
- Bello (bel-lo) means gorgeous (male).
- Thank you very much (grah-see-eh mee-leh). Thank you very much.
- Have a good day. Have a pleasant day!

A Word for the Wise

Pronunciation is important! Don't be scared to make errors; Italians respect effort. Most importantly, having some fun with it! A simple grin and polite gesture may go a long way.

Bonus Tip: Install a translation app on your phone for on-the-go help. Many restaurants and stores also offer English menus.

Embrace the journey

Learning a few essential Italian words can enrich your Amalfi Coast trip and provide opportunities for cultural contacts. Imagine how satisfying it is to order a wonderful dinner in Italian, ask for directions like a native, or say, "Grazie!" So pack your luggage, channel your inner Italian, and prepare to dominate talks on the Amalfi Coast!

Chapter 19: Staying Safe and Healthy (Tips and Medical Care)

The Amalfi Coast, towering cliffs, picturesque towns, and active culture entices those seeking an exceptional Italian getaway. While safety is always a top concern on vacation, taking a few steps may help you have a stress-free trip.

Sun Safety:

The Mediterranean sun may be harsh, particularly during the peak summer months. Apply high-SPF sunscreen (30 or above) generously and reapply regularly, particularly after swimming or sweating. Seek shade during the warmest portion of the day (usually between 12 and 4 p.m.), and wear a hat and sunglasses for further protection.

Water Safety:

The Amalfi Coast has beautiful beaches and crystal-clear seas, but it is critical to consider aquatic safety. Swim only on approved beaches with lifeguards. Be mindful of currents and avoid swimming alone, particularly in quiet coves. If you want to explore secret caves or take a boat excursion, ask about life jackets and safety precautions beforehand.

Footwear Matters:

The Amalfi Coast's landscape may be rough, with tiny, cobblestoned streets and steep walkways. Pack sturdy walking shoes or sandals with adequate traction to comfortably negotiate this terrain. Avoid wearing flip-flops or high heels since they might increase the risk of slipping and falling.

Be pickpocket savvy:

Petty theft is possible at every tourist location, particularly in busy places. Protect your belongings by wearing purses or bags across your body and avoiding carrying large quantities of cash. Utilize hotel safes to keep vital papers and valuables secure when not in use.

Respect the environment.

The Amalfi Coast is a natural wonder, and conserving its beauty is critical. Dispose of waste appropriately, prevent littering, and adhere to local environmental standards. Respect established hiking pathways and avoid going off the main path, particularly in landslide-prone regions.

Medical Care:

While medical services are widely accessible along the Amalfi Coast, it is advisable to bring essential prescriptions and consider travel insurance in case of unexpected events. In an emergency, know where the closest pharmacy ("Farmacia") and hospital are. Carry a basic first-aid kit, including bandages, antiseptic wipes, and pain medications.

Embrace the local culture.

A little respect may go a long way. Dress modestly while visiting churches and religious places. Learn simple Italian words to demonstrate respect for the local culture and improve your communication skills with locals. Be aware of noise levels, particularly at night, and avoid disturbing the quiet of the neighbors.

Staying Safe On the Road:

If you want to hire a vehicle to explore the Amalfi Coast, be mindful of the twisting, narrow roads with steep drop-offs. Italian driving tendencies may be forceful, making defensive driving vital. Learn about traffic laws and parking limitations. If you need to gain experience with the region or feel uncomfortable driving across the rugged terrain, consider using public transit or a cab.

Following these easy safety recommendations and using common sense ensures your Amalfi Coast journey is filled with leisure, discovery, and great memories. So pack your bags, relax, and prepare to be enchanted by the beauty of Italy's shoreline.

Part Six: Appendix

Appendix A: Festival and Event Calendar

The Amalfi Coast is more than just a destination for sunbathers and history fans; it's a location that comes alive with exciting festivals and activities all year. There is something for everyone, from religious processions to outdoor cinema screenings. Here's a look at the Amalfi Coast's holiday atmosphere to help you schedule your vacation around these thrilling celebrations:

Spring (March to May):

- **Lemon celebration (Festa del Limone):** Held yearly in communities such as Sorrento and Maiori, this celebration honors the region's renowned citrus fruit. Expect colorful parades, culinary demos with lemon-infused meals, and kiosks filled with local lemon items.

- **The Amalfi Boat Race (Regata delle Repubbliche Marinare)** brings a historic rivalry to life as teams from Amalfi, Pisa, Genoa, and Venice participate in an exciting boat race around the Amalfi Coast.

Summer (June to August):

- **Positano's Landing of the Saracens (Lo Sbarco dei Saraceni):** This spectacular recreation recalls a historical event from 1544 when the town successfully withstood a pirate onslaught. Expect a lively environment with fireworks, music, and costumed participation.

- **Ravello Festival:** Immerse yourself in classical music at this acclaimed festival, which takes place in Ravello's stunning open-air theater. Throughout the summer, renowned orchestras and artists perform onstage.

Autumn (September to November):

- **Salerno Foreign Film Festival:** Moviegoers travel to Salerno for this famous film festival, which showcases both Italian and foreign films. Expect screenings, red-carpet galas, and opportunities to meet film industry superstars.

- **Festival of Sant'Andrea:** This religious event, held on June 27th and November 30th, celebrates Saint Andrew, Amalfi's patron saint. Expect a boisterous parade, traditional music, and fireworks.

Winter (December to February):

- **Christmas Markets:** Quaint Christmas markets convert Amalfi Coast communities into winter wonderlands. Browse handmade decorations, drink warm mulled wine, and enjoy the Christmas ambiance.

- **New Year's Eve:** Celebrate the new year with a bang! Many villages have colorful festivities with fireworks over the breathtaking shoreline.

Beyond the calendar:

This is only a sampling of the various festivals and events held along the Amalfi Coast throughout the year. It is always a good idea to check local event listings and tourist information websites for the most recent news and hidden treasures.

Embrace the festivities.

Participating in a local festival is an excellent opportunity to immerse yourself in Amalfi Coast culture and customs. So, plan your vacation around an event that interests you, and expect to be carried away by the region's contagious energy and vivid spirit.

ID | Tara D. Hayes

Appendix B: Maps of the Amalfi Coast.

Printed in Great Britain
by Amazon